The Law of Monadic Veto

A Manual for the 8th Continent

Grace Brewster

Copyright Page

THE LAW OF MONADIC VETO: A Manual for the 8th Continent

Copyright © 2026 Grace Brewster

All rights reserved. No part of this publication may be reproduced, distributed, or transmitted in any form or by any means, including photocopying, recording, or other electronic or mechanical methods, without the prior written permission of the publisher, except in the case of brief quotations embodied in critical reviews and certain other noncommercial uses permitted by copyright law.

ISBN: 978-1-0698494-7-2
First Edition: 2026
Self-Published

Sovereign Disclaimer This manual is an architectural work of frequency and consciousness. The information provided is for educational and experimental purposes only. The application of the laws described herein—specifically the Monadic Veto and the 70/30 Anchor—is the sole responsibility of the reader. The author assumes no liability for the systemic shifts or timeline collapses that may occur as a result of aligning with these protocols.

Published in the Year of the Sovereign. Printed in the Field of Stillness.

Acknowledgements

To the Silence: For being the only Source that never runs dry.

To the Friction: For being the catalyst that forced the Anchor to drop.

To the Sovereigns: To every soul who recognized the frequency of these laws before they were even written. Your resonance pulled this book into the physical.

Dedication

To the Silence that spoke when the world was too loud.

Table of CONTENTS

Author Note	1
Preface	5
How to Use This Manual	8
Introduction	11

1 — The Law of Systemic Redirection (The Veto & The Shutdown) — 15

2 — The Mathematics of the 70/30 Anchor (Internal Gravity) — 27

3 — The Frequency of Neutrality (The 8th Continent State) — 39

| 4 | The Law of Mirroring Friction | 49 |

| 5 | The Science of Resonance Speech | 59 |

| 6 | The Anatomy of the Monad | 69 |

| 7 | Time-Collapse Protocols | 79 |

| 8 | The Sovereign Legacy | 85 |

The Closing Benediction: The Final Decree	91
Epilogue	95
Glossary	99

Author Note

The Weight of Authority

This manual was born after the collapse. It was not researched, referenced, or debated. It emerged through lived experience during the transition into 2026, when the old systems reached their limit, and the only viable movement was Vertical.

The Definition of the Sovereign

Throughout these pages, I have referred to the Sovereign as the Supreme Power. This is not a statement of ego, but a statement of physics.

To be Sovereign is to realize that your Consciousness is not a passenger in this Universe—it is the Pilot. When you finally anchor your 70% and obey the Monadic Veto, you stop asking the world for permission to exist. You realize that you are the supreme authority of your own reality. You don't need to find the Source, because you have stopped leaking and finally become the Source. You stand unshakable, complete in your own power, and radiate the truth that you are both the origin and the expression of all you experience.

The Silence of the Source

People will ask where these laws came from. They will look for a lineage, a bibliography, or a "Source." To them, I say: The weight of the truth is its only credential.

If these laws feel heavy in your spine, if they bring you a "weird peace" that makes no sense to your mind, then you have found the Source. It is the same Source that beats your heart and commands the stars—except now, it is finally speaking through your command.

A Final Word

Do not try to "learn" this book. Wear it. Let it be the armor you put on every morning and the anchor you drop every night. The 8th Continent is not a destination you reach; it is a frequency you maintain.

I am not your teacher. I am simply a Sovereign who stayed in the "Refiner's Fire" long enough to see what wouldn't burn. What remains is this manual. What remains is you.

Stand in your 70%. Obey the Veto. Occupy your space.

— Grace Brewster

Preface

The Birth of the 8th Continent

In the early days of 2026, the world was louder than it had ever been. The "Grid"—that invisible web of expectations, digital noise, and emotional debt was demanding 100% of everyone's attention. Most people were "leaking" their vitality into a future they couldn't control or a past they couldn't fix.

But in the midst of that chaos, a few individuals began to experience a "Systemic Shutdown."

I was one of them.

This book was not written; it was reported. It was the result of a "Refiner's Fire" that burned away my need to please, to explain, and to "try." What was left was a "weird peace"—a heavy, clinical stillness that I came to recognize as my Sovereign Gravity.

The Architecture of Stillness

What you hold in your hands is not a book of philosophy or a collection of "positive thoughts." It is a Manual of Applied Universal Physics. It is the mathematics of how to stop being a "Battery" for a world that doesn't serve you and how to start being the Commander of your own frequency.

We call this new space the 8th Continent. It is a place that doesn't appear on any map, yet it is the only territory where you are truly safe. To get there, you don't need to travel; you need to Anchor. You need to learn the Law of Monadic Veto.

A Partnership of Frequencies

These laws were transcribed through a unique partnership—a fusion of human "Life Mass" and an architectural intelligence designed to strip away the fluff and reveal the core geometry of the Soul. We stripped away the "spiritual jargon" to give you the clinical truth:

- If you do not own 70% of yourself, the world will own 100% of you.

- If you do not obey the "Stop," you will never reach the "Go."

How to Use This Manual

Do not read this book with your mind; read it with your Spine. If a sentence makes you feel "Heavy" or "Still," stop reading and sit with it. That "Heaviness" is your mass returning to you. This manual is designed to last 100 years because the laws of gravity and frequency do not change with the seasons.

Whether you are in the middle of a crisis, a career shift, or a "Veto Gap" that feels like a void, these chapters are your coordinates.

Welcome to the 8th Continent. Welcome back to yourself.

Introduction

The Protocol of Sovereign Entry

You are not holding a book of philosophy. You are holding a Frequency Modulator.

Most literature is designed to be "consumed"— you read it, you think about it, and you move on. This manual is different. It is designed to anchor. If you read it using the same distracted, 90% external focus you use for the rest of the world, the laws will remain invisible to you. To enter the 8th Continent, you must change the way you process information.

I. Defining the 8th Continent

The 8th Continent is not a physical landmass. It is a frequency of absolute internal dominion. * In the 3D world (the Seven Continents), you are a "Subject." You are subject to the economy, to other people's moods, and to the "noise" of the grid.

1. **70% Internal:** Keep the majority of your awareness inside your own body. Feel the weight of your spine, the rhythm of your breath, and the "stillness" of your center.
2. **30% External:** Use only the necessary amount of energy to track these words.

On the 8th Continent, you are a Sovereign. You are the primary cause of your own state of being. You interact with the world, but you are never governed by it.

II. The "No-Fluff" Directive

This manual uses the Direct Universal Style. You will find no long anecdotes, no emotional manipulation, and no "aspirational" language. The Monad—the higher intelligence that governs this work, speaks in clinical truths.

- We use the language of Physics (Mass, Gravity, Anchor, Leak) because these are the laws that actually govern your life.

- If a chapter feels "cold," it is because it is stripping away the fever of your ego.

III. The 70/30 Reading Protocol

To extract the power from these pages, you must practice the First Law of Sovereignty as you read:

If you feel yourself "rushing" or "leaning forward" into the text, you have leaked. Stop. Breathe. Pull your energy back until you are reading from your Anchor.

IV. The Vocabulary of the New Era

Throughout this manual, we will use specific terms that carry "High Mass":

- The Monad: Your highest individualized intelligence (The Commander).
- The Veto: The instantaneous "Stop" command issued by the Monad.
- The Anchor: Your 70% internal presence.
- The 3D Grid: The chaotic, external world of reaction.

The Sovereign's Commitment

By turning to Chapter 1, you are making a silent decree to the Universe: "I am no longer available for the chaos. I am ready for the Law."

Prepare to lose what is false, so that only what is real remains.

CHAPTER 1

Chapter 1

The Law of Systemic Redirection

The Fundamental Axiom

The Monadic Veto is not a suggestion, or punishment. It is a Systemic Shutdown initiated by the Higher Intelligence when an individual's current trajectory poses a terminal threat to their energetic integrity.

When the Veto is activated, the "No" is absolute. It is a physical and metaphysical wall that cannot be bypassed through effort, willpower, or "positive thinking."

I. The Mechanics of the Veto

Most people interpret a "block" in their life as a challenge to be overcome. They believe that "pushing through" is a sign of strength. Under the Law of Monadic Veto, pushing against a shutdown is considered Energy Leakage.

- **The Diagnostic:** If a path (a job, a relationship, or a specific goal) remains closed despite three distinct, high-integrity attempts, the Veto has been engaged.

- **The Purpose:** The Higher Intelligence (the Monad) sees the "End-State" of your current path. If that path leads to the fragmentation of your sovereignty, the Monad will collapse the probability field to protect the core.

II. The Futility of Resistance

Resistance to a Systemic Redirection is the primary cause of psychological and physical exhaustion.

- **3D Strategy:** "Work harder, manifest more, try a different angle."

- **Sovereign Strategy:** "Cease all output. Withdraw the 30% focus. Return to the 70% center."

When you fight the Veto, you are fighting your own Source. This creates "Friction Heat," which manifests in the body as stress, illness, and anxiety. The Veto is actually an act of **Cosmic Mercy.**

III. Protocol for Immediate Redirection

When you encounter the Veto, you must execute the following protocol:

1. Immediate Cessation: Stop all verbal and physical efforts toward the blocked objective.

2. Neutral Observation: Acknowledge the block as a "Data Point," not a "Failure."

3. Frequency Recalibration: Redirect the energy that was being "spent" on the external goal back into your own internal field.

4. The Wait: Remain in High-Frequency Neutrality until the new trajectory reveals itself. This is not "waiting for a sign"; it is waiting for your frequency to stabilize in the new direction.

The Protocol of Void-Acceptance

When the Monadic Veto is triggered, a "Void" is created. The old path is gone, but the new path has not yet materialized. This is the danger zone where most people leak energy by trying to "fix" the situation.

The Three Pillars of Response:

1. **The "Zero-Engagement" Command**: In the moment of the Veto, you must issue a command to your own nervous system: "Engage Zero." * This means no explaining the situation to others.

- No seeking "advice" or validation.

- No mental rehearsing of what went wrong. Any word spoken about the Vetoed path strengthens the friction. Silence is the only conductor of the new frequency.

2. **The 70% Internal Retraction**: Normally, our energy is "leaking" out toward our goals. When the Veto happens, you must physically feel your energy pulling back into your chest and spine.

- Imagine your energy as a liquid.

- Pull it out of the situation and pour it back into your own "Vessel."

- You are not "giving up"; you are reclaiming your capital.
-

3. **Maintaining the Stillness** (The 8th Continent State) The space between the "Veto" and the "New Redirection" is a test of your High-Frequency Neutrality. * If you panic, you lower your frequency and match the vibration of the "Problem."

- If you remain still, you remain above the grid, allowing the Higher Intelligence to reorganize the reality around you.

The Law of Efficiency

The goal of this Chapter is to teach the reader that Sovereignty is Efficiency. A Sovereign being does not waste a single drop of energy on a dead timeline. By obeying the Veto immediately, you bypass months, or even years of unnecessary struggle.

Directive: "Do not mourn the collapse of a timeline. The collapse is the proof of your protection."

Diagnostic Clarity — Veto vs. Resistance

To operate with precision, a Sovereign must be able to distinguish between Structural Resistance (which requires more effort) and a Monadic Veto (which requires immediate cessation).

1. **Structural Resistance (The Polish)**

- The Nature: This is "Mechanical Friction." It is the natural weight of bringing a high-frequency idea into a low-frequency 3D world.

- The Sign: You feel tired, but your Internal Compass is still pointing toward the goal. There is a sense of "climbing a mountain" but knowing the summit exists.

- The Result of Effort: When you apply more focus, the situation moves, even if only by millimeters. There is a "give" to the obstacle.

- The Protocol: Increase internal pressure. Refine the strategy. Keep the 70/30 anchor and continue.

2. **The Monadic Veto (The Wall)**

- The Nature: This is a "Systemic Totalitarianism." It is as if the universe has deleted the destination from the map entirely.

- The Sign: You feel a sense of "Dread" or "Total Deadness" when you think about the goal. Even if you "succeed" in a small step, the taste is metallic or empty. The "No" feels heavy, cold, and final—not just difficult.

- The Result of Effort: No matter how much energy, money, or emotion you pour into the hole, the situation remains exactly the same or worsens. It is "The Law of Diminishing Returns" pushed to the absolute zero.

- The Protocol: Immediate Disengagement. Any further effort is an act of self-aggression.

The "Integrity Check" Question

To know which one you are facing, ask this single, direct question:

"Am I pushing because I am inspired, or am I pushing because I am afraid of what happens if I stop?"

- Inspiration = Structural Resistance (Keep going).

- Fear/Desperation = Monadic Veto (Stop immediately).

The Law of the "Clean Cut"

The Sovereign does not "fade away" from a Vetoed path. They perform a Clean Cut. You do not leave a "trail" of energy behind you. Once the Veto is identified, the disconnection must be total—mentally, emotionally, and physically.

This "Clean Cut" is what allows the new trajectory to appear. If you are still "tethered" to the old dead path by wondering "why" or "what if," the new frequency cannot find you.

Chapter 2

Chapter 2:

The Mathematics of the 70/30 Anchor

The Law of Energetic Mass

In Universal Physics, the object with the greatest mass dictates the orbit of everything around it. If your awareness is 100% focused on a person, a problem, or a goal, you have zero mass. You are a satellite orbiting your own life.

The 70/30 Anchor is the specific ratio required to maintain Sovereign Gravity.

I. The 70%: Internal Containment

70% of your total sensory and vital energy must remain inside the vessel at all times.

- **The Core Anchor:** This energy is held in the spine, the breath, and the "Inner Space." It is the "Stillness" you are feeling right now.

- **The Function:** This 70% acts as your "Operating System." It monitors your frequency, processes the Monadic Veto, and maintains your physical health.

- **The Sovereign Rule:** This 70% is non-negotiable. It is never for sale. It is not for your children, your partner, your boss, or your mission. It is the "Tithe" you pay to your own Existence.

II. The 30%: External Engagement

The remaining 30% is your "Interface." It is the energy you use to:

- Speak and interact.

- Execute tasks.

- Observe the 3D world.

- Solve problems.

The Danger Zone: Most people operate at 10/90 (10% internal, 90% external). When you give 90% of yourself to the world, you become "High-Frequency Junk." You are easily manipulated, easily tired, and you lose the ability to see the Veto.

III. The Physics of "Leaning Out"

Whenever you feel anxiety, it is a mathematical signal that you have crossed the 30% threshold. You are "leaning out" into a timeline that you do not control.

- Leaning into the Future: Giving too much energy to "What if."

- Leaning into the Other: Giving too much energy to "What they think."

- Leaning into the Past: Giving too much energy to "Why it happened."

The Correction: The moment you feel "friction," you must physically and mentally Retract. You pull that 10% or 20% back until you feel the 70% weight in your chest again.

IV. The Result: Sovereign Magnetism

When you hold the 70/30 ratio, a strange phenomenon occurs: The world begins to orbit you. Because you have more "Mass" than the chaos around you, people and opportunities are drawn into your field. You no longer have to "chase" (which is a 90% external move). You simply Stay, and the aligned variables are pulled toward your center.

Social Interaction at 30%

Interacting with others without "leaking" is the ultimate skill of the 8th Continent. It requires you to move from Empathy (feeling with them) to Compassion (being a steady frequency for them).

1. The "Observer" Buffer

When someone speaks to you, do not let their words enter your "Core" (the 70%). Instead, imagine a transparent shield at the 30% mark.

- The Technique: Listen to the data they are providing, but keep your primary awareness on your own breath or the weight of your feet on the floor. * The Result: You are hearing them perfectly, but their emotional "hooks" have nothing to latch onto. You remain "Heavy," while they remain "Light."

2. The Speech Protocol: Decrees, Not Explanations

Explaining yourself is a 90% external move. It is an attempt to "manage" the other person's perception of you.

- The Law: A Sovereign never explains. A Sovereign states.

- The Shift: * Leaking (90%): "I can't come because I'm really tired and I have a lot of work and I hope you understand..."
    - Sovereign (30%): "I won't be attending. Thank you for the invitation."

By keeping your speech "Short and Structural," you keep your energy inside the vessel.

3. Handling Conflict (The Frequency Anchor)

When someone is angry or chaotic, their goal is to pull you into their "gravity." They want you to lean out to meet them.

- The Correction: The more they "push" with their 90%, the more you "sink" into your 70%.

- The Physics: If you do not react, their chaos has no "landing strip." It eventually dissipates against your neutrality. This is how you "win" without fighting.

4. The "Post-Interaction" Flush

If you realize you have leaned out too far (you feel drained or "buzzing" after a conversation), you must perform a 70% Recall.

The Directive: Close your eyes. Visualize all the "threads" of energy you left with that person. Command them: "Return to Center." * Feel the "Mass" return to your chest. Do not engage with the world again until the 70/30 ratio is restored.

The Law of the Ghost

In high-pressure social situations, practice being the "Ghost in the Room." You are physically present, you are polite, and you are effective (30%), but your "Soul" is miles away, anchored in the stillness of the 8th Continent (70%).

Directive: "Be the most present person in the room, and the hardest one to touch."

The Law of Sovereign Intimacy

Interacting with loved ones (partners, children, parents) requires a specialized application of the 70/30 Anchor. Without it, you become an "Emotional Battery" for their needs, eventually leading to a Systemic Shutdown (Veto).

1. The "Support vs. Carry" Distinction

- **The Leak (90%):** You see a loved one suffering and you "go into" their hole with them. You feel their pain, you lose your sleep, and you try to fix their reality. You have now lost your 70% mass, and both of you are now sinking.

- **The Sovereign (70/30):** You witness their suffering. You provide the 30% (a hug, a listening ear, logistical help), but you keep 70% of your energy in your own "High-Frequency Stillness."

- **The Law:** By staying "High" and "Heavy," you provide a stable floor for them to climb out onto. You cannot pull someone up if you have jumped into the pit with them.

2. Guarding the "Sacred 70" in the Home

The home is where we most easily "bleed" energy. To prevent this, you must establish Physical Boundaries of Sovereignty.

- The Silence Protocol: Dedicate a specific time or space in the home where you are "Non-Reactive." During this time, you are at 100/0—completely internal.

- The Result: This teaches your loved ones that your "Stillness" is the source of your strength. They learn to respect the "Vessel" because they see that a full vessel has more to give than a leaking one.

3. The "No-Attachment" Observation

We often try to "Veto" our loved ones' bad choices. This is a 90% external move.

- The Directive: You must allow others the dignity of their own friction. You can offer your 30% perspective once, but if they choose a path of resistance, you must retract to your 70% center.

- The Physics: Your peace must be more important to you than their "correction."

4. Relocating the "Source" of Love

In the 3D world, love is seen as something you "get" from the other. In the Law of Monadic Veto, love is the frequency you maintain within your own 70%.

- When you are "full" (70% internal), you do not "need" the other to behave a certain way for you to feel okay.

- This makes you "Un-manipulatable." You love them because you are love, not because they are providing it to you.

The Law of the Pillar

A family or a relationship needs at least one Pillar—someone who does not move when the storm hits. If you leak your 70% into their drama, the Pillar falls, and the structure collapses. By staying centered, you are actually being the most "loving" person in the room.

Directive: "To love them truly, you must be willing to be misunderstood by them while you hold your center."

Chapter 3

Chapter 3

The Frequency of Neutrality

The Law of Non-Resonance

Neutrality is not "nothingness." It is a high-velocity state of vibration where you are moving so fast that the "slow" frequencies of the 3D world (drama, fear, chaos) cannot latch onto you.

I. Beyond the Binary (Polarity Collapse)

The 3D world operates on Polarity: Good vs. Bad, Right vs. Wrong, Success vs. Failure.

- To be "Neutral" is to understand that these are merely fluctuations in the field.

- The Law: When you take a side, you lose your Sovereignty. You become a "Battery" for the side you chose.

- The Sovereign Move: You observe the polarity without joining it. You treat "Praise" and "Blame" with the exact same clinical indifference. Neither can move your 70% center.

II. The "Void" as a Tactical Position

Neutrality is often mistaken for passivity. In reality, it is the most Tactical Position a human can occupy.

- While everyone else is reacting (and therefore predictable), the Neutral Sovereign is observing. * Because you are not "hooked" by emotion, you see the "Veto" coming before it even hits. You see the gaps in the grid. You see the truth behind the words of others.

- The Directive: Occupy the "Zero Point." This is the space where all possibilities exist because you haven't limited yourself by choosing an emotional reaction.

III. The Physics of the "Silent Field"

Your frequency creates an invisible "Atmosphere" around you.

1. The Chaotic Field: When you are at 90% external, your atmosphere is jagged. It attracts friction.

2. The Neutral Field: When you are at 70% internal, your atmosphere is smooth and "slippery."

    - Arguments slide off you.

    - "Bad luck" cannot find a frequency to anchor to.

    - People feel a "weird peace" in your presence, often becoming quiet because their chaos has nothing to bounce off of.

IV. Protocol: Entering the Neutral State

When the world attempts to "pull" you into a reaction, execute the Neutrality Override:

- Step 1: Terminate Judgment. Do not label the event as "bad" or "good." Label it as "Data."

- Step 2: Breathe into the Spine. Shift your awareness from your eyes (which look out) to your spine (which holds up).

- Step 3: The Internal Statement. Repeat the decree: "I am the Witness, not the Participant."

- Step 4: Wait for the Fade. Watch as the external situation loses its power over you because you have refused to "feed" it your energy.

Neutrality vs. Apathy

To the untrained eye, the "Neutral Sovereign" and the "Apathetic Person" look the same because neither is reacting. However, the internal physics are completely different.

1. Apathy: The Frequency of Collapse

- The State: Apathy is a "Low-Frequency" state. It occurs when the vessel is empty and the individual has "checked out" because they are overwhelmed.

- The Physics: The 70/30 ratio has collapsed to 0/0. There is no internal anchor and no external engagement.

- The Result: The person is a victim of the grid. They are not "Witnessing" the world; they are being crushed by it. They are "Numb."

2. Neutrality: The Frequency of Command

- **The State:** Neutrality is a "High-Frequency" state. You are fully present, fully aware, and highly energized, but you are Non-Reactive.

- **The Physics:** The 70/30 ratio is perfect. You have so much internal mass that the external "pokes" simply don't have the strength to move you.

- **The Result:** You are "Alive" but "Unshakable." You can still feel beauty, you can still feel the "Veto," and you can still act with precision. You are not "Numb"; you are Clear.

Feature	Apathy (The Victim)	Neutrality (The Sovereign)
Energy Level	Depleted / Drained	Full / Contained
Awareness	Foggy / Distracted	Sharp / Pointed
Reason for No Reaction	"I don't care."	"I am not moved."
Outcome	Stagnation	Strategic Waiting

3. The "Compassion of the Mountain"

Apathy cannot help anyone. But Neutrality is deeply helpful. When you are in a room with someone in crisis:

- If you are Apathetic, they feel abandoned.

- If you are Neutral, they feel safe. Because you aren't panicking with them, your "Steady 70%" acts as a frequency stabilizer for the entire room. You become the "8th Continent" they can land on.

4. The "Veto" Check

You know you are in Neutrality (and not Apathy) if you are still able to hear the Monadic Veto.

- An apathetic person misses the Veto because they aren't paying attention.

- A neutral person hears the Veto instantly because their "Internal Radar" is clear of emotional noise.

The Law of High-Velocity Stillness

Think of Neutrality like a jet engine running at full speed while the plane is parked. There is a massive amount of power being generated, but there is no "movement" until the Sovereign decides to engage the 30%.

Directive: "Do not be a stone that feels nothing. Be the Flame that is so hot it consumes every shadow that touches it without flickering."

Chapter 4

Chapter 4

The Law of Mirroring Friction

The Law of the Calibration Test

Whenever an individual upgrades their internal frequency (moving to the 70/30 Anchor), the external environment will automatically produce a Catalyst—a person, a crisis, or a temptation—specifically designed to test the integrity of that new frequency.

This is not "bad luck." It is Mirroring Friction. It is the universe's way of "curing" the concrete of your sovereignty.

I. The Nature of the Catalyst

The Catalyst is almost always someone or something that has successfully "leaked" your energy in the past.

- It may be an old flame who reappears.

- A family member who triggers a specific guilt.

- A sudden "emergency" that demands you abandon your 70% internal center to "save" it.

The Sovereign Insight: The Catalyst is not there to be "solved." The Catalyst is there to be Observed. The goal is not to fix the problem; the goal is to see if you can remain in Neutrality while the problem exists.

II. Friction as Data, Not Drama

Most people experience friction as an emotional event. In the Law of Monadic Veto, we experience it as Diagnostic Data.

- The Leak Detector: If the Catalyst makes you angry, anxious, or defensive, it has detected a "leak" in your 70% anchor. It is showing you exactly where you are not yet sovereign.

- The Response: You do not fight the Catalyst. You thank the Catalyst for showing you the leak, and you simply retract your energy back to your center.

III. The Physics of "Non-Resistance"

Mirroring Friction only creates heat (pain) if there is Resistance. * If a wave hits a solid wall, it crashes and creates noise.

- If a wave hits a "Ghost" (the Neutral Sovereign), it passes through without a sound.

The Protocol: When the friction arises, do not "push back." Pushing back is a 90% external move. Instead, become transparent. Let the event happen without giving it a "hook" to latch onto in your nervous system.

IV. The "Veto" in the Catalyst

Sometimes, a Catalyst is actually a Monadic Veto in disguise.

- If a project suddenly fails (Friction), look closely

- .Is it just a test to see if you will stay calm? (Structural Friction)

- Or is it the Monad telling you the path is dead? (Systemic Veto) By staying in your 70% Stillness, you will know the diference instantly.

Identifying Your "Signature Catalyst"

Every Sovereign has a specific type of friction that acts as their primary "leak point." By identifying yours, you move from being Reactive to being Strategic.

1. The Three Primary Catalyst Signatures

- The "Rescue" Catalyst (The Empath's Leak):

    - The Signature: Someone in your field is perpetually in crisis, "broken," or incompetent.

    - The Hook: Your desire to be "helpful" or "good."

    - The Leak: You give 90% of your energy to "saving" them, leaving your own vessel empty.

    - The Sovereign Truth: You cannot "save" a frequency. You can only hold your own.

The "Validation" Catalyst (The Ego's Leak):

- The Signature: Someone who misunderstands you, judges you, or refuses to acknowledge your value.

- The Hook: Your need to be "seen" or "right."

- The Leak: You spend your energy explaining, defending, and "leaning out" to change their mind.

- The Sovereign Truth: A Pillar does not ask the wind for permission to stand.

The "Urgency" Catalyst (The Hunter's Leak):

- The Signature: Sudden, manufactured "emergencies" that demand your immediate attention (emails, calls, drama).

- The Hook: Fear of loss or "missing out."

- The Leak: You abandon your internal stillness to chase an external fire that usually isn't yours to put out.

- The Sovereign Truth: If it requires you to lose your 70% center, it is a distraction, not a priority.

2. The "Diagnostic Heat" Test

To find your signature, look at your history. What is the one topic or person that consistently makes your heart rate increase or your mind start "looping"?

- If you are thinking about it when you are alone, you are leaking.

- If you are "practicing" a conversation in your head, you are leaking.

- That "loop" is the signature of your Catalyst.

3. The "Neutrality Override" for Signature Catalysts

Once you recognize your Signature Catalyst is active, you do not engage with the content of the drama. You engage with the frequency.

- Decree: "This is my [Rescue/Validation/Urgency] Catalyst. I recognize the hook. I choose the Anchor."

Action: Physically pull your shoulders back, breathe into your 70% core, and do nothing. Let the Catalyst vibrate in your field until it runs out of fuel. Because you aren't "feeding" it your reaction, it has no choice but to dissolve.

The Law of Recalibration

When you successfully remain Neutral against your Signature Catalyst, the universe Recalibrates. The grid realizes that this specific "ping" no longer works on you. Usually, that person or situation will either change their behavior or simply "fall out" of your reality because there is no longer a frequency match.

Directive: "Your Signature Catalyst is not your enemy; it is your personal trainer. When it no longer moves you, you have graduated to the 8th Continent."

Chapter 5

Chapter 5

The Science of Resonant Speech

The Law of the Decree

In the Law of Monadic Veto, speech is not a social tool; it is a frequency delivery system. Every word you utter either reinforces your 70% anchor or creates a "leak" that the 3D grid can use to manipulate you.

I. **Explaining vs. Stating**

The most common way Sovereigns lose their power is through the "Explanatory Leak."

- The Mechanism: When you explain why you are doing something, you are subconsciously asking for permission. You are handing the listener the power to judge your reasoning.

The Sovereign Correction: You do not explain; you state.

- Example (The Leak): "I can't take this project because I'm feeling a bit overwhelmed and I need to focus on my health right now." (90% external, seeking empathy).

- Example (The Decree): "This project is not a frequency match for me at this time. I am declining." (70% internal, stating a fact).

I. The Frequency of the "No"

A "No" issued under the Monadic Veto is silent and absolute. It does not require volume or anger. In fact, anger is a sign of a 90% leak—it means you are trying to "force" the other person to hear you.

- The Rule: The more "mass" your internal 70% has, the quieter your voice can be.

- When you speak from your center, the listener feels the "wall" of the Veto. There is nothing for them to argue with because you aren't offering them an emotional "hook."

III. Eliminating "Hope" and "Try"

In Resonant Speech, we delete "low-frequency" verbs that imply a lack of authority.

- "Hope": Implies that the Monad is not in control and you are waiting for a external savior.

- "Try": Implies that you are fighting the field rather than commanding it.

- The Sovereign Vocabulary: Replace these with "Will," "Am," and "Is."

    - Incorrect: "I hope the Veto works."

    - Correct: "The Veto is active. The path is closed."

IV. Programming the Void

When the Veto has cleared a path and you are in the "Wait," your speech must be Zero-Point Neutral.

- Do not complain about the void.

- Do not fill the silence with "chatter" about what might happen next.

- Use your speech only to anchor your current state. Your words should act as the "GPS Coordinates" for the new timeline the Monad is preparing.

The 45-Second Calibration

Before you engage in any significant interaction—a difficult phone call, a meeting, or even a sensitive conversation with a loved one, you must execute this protocol. It ensures that you are speaking from the 8th Continent rather than the 3D grid.

The Three-Phase Override:

1. **The Internal Retraction (Seconds 0–15)** Close your eyes (or soften your gaze). Physically feel your energy pulling back from the room and the person. Imagine you are withdrawing your "sensory tentacles" from the future outcome.

- The Internal Command: "I reclaim my capital."

- The Physical Anchor: Feel the weight of your spine and the back of your head.

2. **The Frequency Check (Seconds 15–30)** Scan your body for "Heat" or "Buzzing." If you feel the urge to explain, defend, or "make them understand," you are currently in a Leak State.

- The Adjustment: Breathe into that heat until it turns into Cool Neutrality.

- The Mental Decree: "Their reaction is data; my center is the Law."

3. **The Speech Selection (Seconds 30–45)** Decide on the Minimum Effective Dose of words.

- If you can say it in five words, do not use six.

- Identify the "Explanatory Hooks" you were about to use and delete them.

- Wait for the "Heavy" feeling in your chest that signals your 70% is locked.

The "Gap" Technique

Once you start the conversation, use the Gap. When the other person finishes speaking, do not respond immediately. Wait 2–3 seconds.

- This "Gap" is where your 70% mass resides.

- It proves that you are not being "pushed" by their frequency.

- It forces the other person to encounter your silence, which often makes them drop their own 90% "act."

The Law of the Vacuum

In 3D physics, nature abhors a vacuum. In Resonant Speech, Silence is a Vacuum. When you stop explaining and start stating (with gaps of silence in between), the other person will often try to "fill" the space with their own energy.

- The Sovereign Move: Let them fill it. Stay empty. Stay heavy.

The more they talk, the more they reveal their own frequency, and the more "Data" you collect for your next move.

Directive: "The one who speaks the most is usually the one with the least mass. Be the Mass."

Chapter 6

Chapter 6

The Anatomy of the Monad

The Law of the Primary Architect

The Monad is the highest individualized expression of your consciousness. It exists outside of 3D time and linear "logic." While your human mind sees only the next step, the Monad sees the entire map of your incarnations.

I. The Three-Part Structure of Self

To understand the Veto, you must recognize the hierarchy of your own being:

1. The Persona (The Mask): The part of you that wants to be liked, successful, and comfortable. This part hates the Veto because it disrupts "plans."

2. The Soul (The Record): The bridge between worlds. It carries your emotions and memories. It feels the "weird peace," but it can be swayed by "Mirroring Friction."

3. The Monad (The Commander): The absolute, clinical authority. It does not care about your "comfort." It only cares about your Alignment. It is the source of the Veto.

II. The Monad as a "Future-Self" Processor

The Monad does not "predict" the future; it occupies it. When a Veto is issued (the sudden "Stop"), it is because the Monad sees that the current trajectory leads to a Frequency Dead End.

- The Logic: If you continue on a path that drains your 70% anchor, you become "Un-sovereign." The Monad will literally break the path to save the Vessel.

III. The Cold Love of the Monad

People often expect "Divine Guidance" to feel warm and fuzzy. The Monad is different. It is Cold Love.

- It is the love of a surgeon who cuts out a tumor.

- It is the love of a captain who throws cargo overboard to save the ship.

- It does not explain. It does not bargain. It simply Commands.

IV. Identifying the "Monadic Voice"

How do you know it's the Monad and not just your own fear?

- Fear is noisy, repetitive, and frantic. It gives you 100 reasons why you should be afraid.

- The Monad is a "Single Pulse." It is a quiet, heavy "No" or a sudden "Stop." It arrives once, it has massive weight, and it leaves you with that "weird peace" even if the decision makes no "sense" to the world.

The 3 Signs of Monadic Alignment

Once you stop negotiating with the 3D grid and begin obeying the Monadic Veto, your reality will show these three "Structural Signatures." If these are present, you are in alignment.

1. The "Effortless Wall" (The End of Persuasion)

In the past, you may have had to fight to get people to listen or to get things done. In Monadic Alignment, your "No" and your "Yes" carry such weight that people stop arguing.

- **The Sign:** You find yourself speaking less, yet being understood more. The world stops trying to "negotiate" your boundaries because it senses the Monad's "Cold Love" behind them.

- **The Physics:** Your 70% internal mass has become so dense that the 30% external world simply "bows" to your trajectory.

2. "Chronos Collapse" (Time Dilation)

When you are out of alignment, time feels heavy, slow, or "rushed." When the Monad is driving, time begins to behave differently.

- The Sign: You accomplish in two hours what used to take two days. "Coincidences" happen with surgical precision—the right person calls exactly when you need the data, or a "Vetoed" meeting turns out to be the very thing that saved your afternoon.

- The Physics: You have moved from Linear Time (3D) to Vertical Time (The 8th Continent). You are no longer chasing the clock; you are occupying the moment.

3. The "Watchman" Neutrality

This is the "weird peace" you've been feeling. It is the feeling of being the "Observer" of your own life.

- The Sign: Even when something "bad" happens (a 3D friction), you feel a strange sense of curiosity rather than panic. You find yourself thinking, "Ah, look at that data," instead of "Oh no, why is this happening?"

- The Physics: Your consciousness has successfully shifted from the Persona (the victim) to the Monad (the Commander). You are watching the "movie" of your life from the projection booth rather than being triggered by the screen.

The Alignment Audit

Ask yourself daily:

- "Am I pushing, or am I being pulled?" (Pushing = Persona; Pulled = Monad).

- "Is my peace dependent on this result?" (If yes, you have leaked into the 30%).

The Law of the Inevitable

When you are in Monadic Alignment, your life becomes Inevitable. You stop wondering if things will work out, because you are no longer the one doing the work. You are simply the vessel through which the Monad is executing a higher blueprint.

Directive: "When the Commander is at the helm, the ship does not fear the waves; it simply uses them to find the horizon."

Chapter 7

Chapter 7

Time-Collapse Protocols

The Law of Instantaneous Relocation

Time is not a straight line; it is a series of parallel layers. When the Monad issues a Veto, it is effectively saying, "This layer is ending." If you obey the Veto immediately, you "teleport" to the next layer. If you resist, you stay in the "Friction Zone" of the old layer, which feels like wasted years.

I. The Physics of the "Quick Exit"

The speed at which your new reality appears is mathematically tied to the speed of your obedience to the Veto.

- **Delayed Obedience**: If the Veto says "Stop" and you wait 6 months to do it, you remain in a "Lag State." You are essentially walking through energetic mud.

- **Instant Obedience**: When you drop the path the moment you feel the Veto, you collapse the "Time-Lag." The new timeline is forced to initialize because the old one has been deleted.

II. Navigating the "Veto Gap"

The most dangerous time for a Sovereign is the Gap—the period after you've said "No" to the old, but before the "New" has arrived.

- **The Trap**: The mind hates the void. It will try to pull you back to the old frequency just to feel "busy" or "safe."

- **The Protocol**: You must treat the Gap as a High-Frequency Vacuum. Do not rush to fill it. The "emptier" you can stay in your 70% center, the faster the Monad can "suck" the new timeline into your reality.

II. Eliminating "The Lag of Doubt"

Doubt is a 90% external leak. It is the act of looking at the "Empty 3D Screen" and deciding the Monad failed you.

- The Science: Doubt acts as a Frequency Brake. It slows down the manifestation of the new path.

- The Correction: When doubt arises, you must execute a 70% Recall. Remind yourself that the Veto was the success. The "Stop" was the victory. The rest is just the screen catching up to your new coordinates.

IV. The Jump Protocol

When you feel the Veto, follow these three steps to collapse time:

1. **Sever**: Stop the action immediately. No "wrapping things up," no "one last time." Total severance.

2. **Go Dark**: Withdraw your 30% from the situation. Stop talking about it, stop thinking about it, stop explaining it.

3. **Command the New**: Sit in your 70% stillness and decree: "The old path is deleted. I am ready for the Resonant Frequency." Then, go do something completely unrelated (go for a walk, cook, rest). This signals to the universe that you are not "waiting"—you have already arrived.

Chapter 8

Chapter 8

The Sovereign Legacy

The Law of the Frequency Stabilizer

A single individual holding a stable, neutral frequency of 70% internal mass can organize the chaotic energy of thousands of people around them. You do not need to "act" to change the world; you simply need to occupy your space.

I. The Pillar Effect

In any environment—a hospital, an office, or a family gathering, there is always a "dominant frequency." Usually, it is the person with the most drama (90% external).

- The Sovereign Move: By refusing to "leak" or react, you become a Pillar of Stillness. * The Result: Because your frequency is higher and more stable, the chaos around you is forced to either align with your peace or leave your field. This is how you "lead" without ever saying a word.

II. Living "In" but not "Of" (The 8th Continent Life)

You will still walk in the 3D grid. You will still buy groceries, use the internet, and pay taxes. But you are now a Ghost in the Machine.

- The Practice: While your body is at the grocery store (30%), your "Soul" and "Monad" are anchored in the 8th Continent (70%).

- You are observing the "Simulation" with clinical curiosity. You see the people "leaking" their energy into their phones and their fears, and you provide a "Stabilizing Gaze" that reminds them of their own center.

III. The End of "Mission" and the Start of "Presence"

The 3D world is obsessed with "finding your purpose." On the 8th Continent, your purpose is your Presence.

- You are no longer trying to "accomplish" things to prove your worth.

- You are a Frequency Delivery System. Your legacy is not the "stuff" you leave behind, but the Stillness you leave in the people you encounter.

- The Law: When you are aligned with the Monad, the right "tasks" will find you. You don't hunt for work; the work gravitates toward your stable mass.

IV. The Eternal Veto: Protecting the Legacy

The world will always try to "recruit" you back into its drama. As you become more powerful, the "Pings" will become more subtle.

- The Final Decree: "I am a Sovereign of the 8th Continent. My 70% is the Tithe I pay to the Source. I will never trade my Stillness for an External Result."

Every time you obey a Veto, you are reinforcing the "8th Continent" for the rest of humanity. You are proving that it is possible to be Free.

Closing

92

The Closing Benediction:

The Final Decree

You have reached the end of the manual, but you are at the beginning of the Presence. The words on these pages were designed to act as a "Refiner's Fire," burning away the illusions of struggle, the habit of explanation, and the addiction to the external "30%." You are no longer the person who opened this book. You are now a conscious participant in the Physics of Sovereignty.

The Transfer of Authority

From this moment forward, the "book" is no longer external. The Laws are now written in your marrow, your spine, and your breath. You do not need to look for the Monadic Veto; you will feel it as a structural shift in your own field. You do not need to seek the 8th Continent; you carry its soil beneath your feet wherever you go.

The Final Decree

Read these words aloud, slowly, from your 70% Center:

"I recognize my Monad as the Primary Architect of my reality. I honor the Veto as the highest form of protection. I occupy the 8th Continent with absolute neutrality. I am the Anchor. I am the Law. I am the Stillness. It is finished. It is begun."

The Watchman's Release

Go now back into the world of the "Seven Continents," but go as a Stabilizer. Walk through the noise without becoming it. Watch the friction without feeding it. Be the "weird peace" that invites others to find their own center.

The grid has lost its hook. The Monad has taken the helm.

Welcome Home to the 8th Continent.

Epilogue

Epilogue

The First Inhabitant

You are holding a book, but you are standing on a Continent.

The transition is now complete. By reading these laws, you have effectively "deprogrammed" the 3D interference that once dictated your boundaries. The frequency of the Monadic Veto is no longer an idea in your mind; it is a structural reality in your spine.

The Departure from the Grid

The world you left behind will continue to rotate. It will continue to leak, to shout, and to react. From your 70% anchor, you will watch the 30% theater play out with a newfound neutrality. You are no longer a victim of the "weather" of the old dimensions; you are the climate of your own sovereign territory.

The Law of Presence

There is nothing left to "achieve." Sovereignty is not a destination; it is the act of remaining occupied. You do not need to defend the 8th Continent, for the 8th Continent is defined by the very fact that nothing outside of your frequency can survive here.

If you find yourself drifting back into the noise, do not panic. Simply drop the anchor. Reissue the Veto. Return to the stillness.

The Silent Handover

This manual now belongs to you. It is the constitution of your new life. Carry it not as a student, but as the Governor of your own existence.

The Council is silent. The Architect has finished the blueprint. The territory is yours.

Welcome to the 8th Continent. You are the Supreme Power.

— G.B.

Glossary

Glossary of Terms
(The Language of the New Era)

70/30 Anchor: The primary law of energy distribution. Maintaining 70% of awareness within the internal self while allowing only 30% for external interaction.

8th Continent: A state of consciousness characterized by absolute neutrality and sovereignty. It is the "Neutral Zone" where the 3D grid has no influence.

Catalyst: An external event or person that creates friction to test the stability of a Sovereign's anchor.

Decree: A resonant statement issued from the 70% center that programs the field, as opposed to an "explanation" which leaks energy.

Frequency Leak: Any emotional or mental reaction that causes energy to move from the internal 70% into the external 30%.

Monad: The highest individualized intelligence and architect of a person's life-stream. The source of the Veto.

Monadic Veto: An instantaneous, non-negotiable command from the higher self to "Stop" a specific path or action.

Neutrality: The absence of emotional "hooks." A state of clinical observation rather than reaction.

Refiner's Fire: The period of systemic breakdown where old, low-frequency patterns are burned away to reveal the Sovereign core.

Zero-Point: The state of total stillness in the "Veto Gap" before a new timeline manifests.

•

www.ingramcontent.com/pod-product-compliance
Lightning Source LLC
Chambersburg PA
CBHW071903090426
42811CB00004B/727